THE
RISE AND RUIN
OF THE
HOA

GLOBAL WARMING
AND WATER DISPLACEMENT

JAMES B FIGHTMASTER

ARCHWAY
PUBLISHING

Archway Publishing books may be ordered through booksellers or by contacting:

Archway Publishing
1663 Liberty Drive
Bloomington, IN 47403
www.archwaypublishing.com
844-669-3957

ISBN: 978-1-6657-6445-2 (sc)
ISBN: 978-1-6657-6446-9 (e)

Library of Congress Control Number: 2024916639

Print information available on the last page.

Archway Publishing rev. date: 08/12/2024

Preamble: When looking at HOAs they seem so archaic and the rules governing seem so hegemonial.

Homeowners associations (HOAs) have indeed garnered criticism for their often strict rules and regulations governing communities. While some view them as necessary for maintaining property values and community standards, others see them as overly restrictive and outdated.

Whether HOAs will persist into the future depends on various factors, including cultural shifts, legal developments, and societal preferences. Here are a few possibilities:

1. **Continued Existence**: HOAs may continue to thrive in certain areas where residents value the sense of community and the assurance of property standards. As long as there are individuals willing to live in HOA-governed neighborhoods and support their existence, these associations may endure.
2. **Adaptation**: HOAs could evolve to become more flexible and responsive to the needs of residents. This might involve revising overly strict rules, incorporating more democratic decision-making processes, and embracing technology to enhance communication and governance.
3. **Decline**: Alternatively, there could be a decline in the prevalence of HOAs as people become more skeptical of their governance structures and seek alternatives. This could be driven by legal challenges, changes in housing trends, or shifts in societal attitudes towards community living.
4. **Regulatory Changes**: Government regulations could also play a role in shaping the future of HOAs. Stricter oversight or reforms aimed at addressing concerns such as transparency, accountability, and residents' rights could significantly impact how HOAs operate.
5. **New Models**: There might also emerge alternative models of community governance that offer the benefits of collective decision-making without some of the drawbacks associated with traditional HOAs. This could include co-housing communities, cooperative housing arrangements, or decentralized governance structures.

Ultimately, the future of HOAs will likely depend on how well they adapt to changing societal norms and address the concerns of residents. While they may continue to exist in some form, it's possible that they will undergo significant transformations to remain relevant in an evolving housing landscape.

THE BIRTH OF HOMEOWNERS ASSOCIATIONS

In the quaint neighborhoods of mid-20th century America, a new concept was taking root—the homeowners association (HOA). Born out of a desire for orderly communities and shared amenities, HOAs initially promised a utopian vision of suburban living. But beneath this facade of uniformity and regulation lay the seeds of conflict that would later bloom into battles over property rights, individual freedoms, and the very essence of community itself.

The origins of HOAs, tracing their development from the post-World War II era to the present day. It was a time of rapid urbanization and suburban expansion, as returning veterans sought the American dream of homeownership and a slice of pastoral bliss outside the city limits. Enterprising developers seized this opportunity, envisioning carefully planned subdivisions with manicured lawns, tidy sidewalks, and a sense of exclusivity that would appeal to the burgeoning middle class.

The first HOAs emerged as a means to maintain this vision of suburban paradise. They wielded powers granted by legal covenants and restrictions, dictating everything from the color of exterior paint to the height of the grass. Residents willingly surrendered some degree of autonomy in exchange for the promise of communal harmony and increased property values. We can see where the real estate tycoons really came into focus and were the meaning behind the HOAs. With group increased uniformity and property value as a lump mass the tycoons could leverage more bang for their buck depending on the size of not only just a house now but an ownership in a whole neighborhood.

In the quaint neighborhoods of mid-20th century America, a new concept was taking root—the homeowners association (HOA). Born out of a desire for orderly communities and shared amenities, HOAs initially promised a utopian vision of suburban living. But beneath this facade of uniformity and regulation lay the seeds of conflict that would later bloom into battles over property rights, individual freedoms, and the very essence of community itself.

In this chapter, we delve into the origins of HOAs, tracing their development from the post-World War II era to the present day. It was a time of rapid urbanization and suburban expansion, as returning veterans sought the American dream of homeownership and a slice of pastoral bliss outside the city limits. Enterprising developers seized this opportunity, envisioning carefully planned subdivisions with manicured lawns, tidy sidewalks, and a sense of exclusivity that would appeal to the burgeoning middle class.

The first HOAs emerged as a means to maintain this vision of suburban paradise. They wielded powers granted by legal covenants and restrictions, dictating everything from the color of exterior paint to the height of the grass. Residents willingly surrendered some degree of autonomy in exchange for the promise of communal harmony and increased property values.

Yet, even in these formative years, cracks began to appear in the facade of HOA governance. Disputes arose over trivial matters, from the placement of holiday decorations to the ownership of shared amenities. Residents found themselves entangled in a web of rules and regulations, subject to the whims of unelected boards and committees.

As we journey through the early days of HOAs, we uncover the tensions simmering beneath the surface—tensions that would eventually erupt into full-blown conflicts between homeowners seeking to assert their rights and HOAs clinging to their authority. It is a story of idealism and disillusionment, of promises made and broken, and of the unintended consequences of well-intentioned planning.

In the quaint neighborhoods of mid-20th century America, a new concept was taking root—the homeowners association (HOA). Born out of a desire for orderly communities and shared amenities, HOAs initially promised a utopian vision of suburban living. But beneath this facade of uniformity and regulation lay the seeds of conflict that would later bloom into battles over property rights, individual freedoms, and the very essence of community itself.

The origins of HOAs trace back to the post-World War II era, a time marked by rapid urbanization and suburban expansion. Returning veterans sought the American dream of homeownership and a slice of pastoral bliss outside the city limits. Enterprising developers seized this opportunity, envisioning carefully planned subdivisions with manicured lawns, tidy sidewalks, and a sense of exclusivity that would appeal to the burgeoning middle class.

The first HOAs emerged as a means to maintain this vision of suburban paradise. They wielded powers granted by legal covenants and restrictions, dictating everything from the color of exterior paint to the height of the grass. Residents willingly surrendered some degree of autonomy in exchange for the promise of communal harmony and increased property values. Behind the scenes, real estate tycoons recognized the potential for increased uniformity and property value, leveraging the collective appeal of a neighborhood to enhance their profits.

However, even in these formative years, cracks began to appear in the facade of HOA governance. Disputes arose over trivial matters, from the placement of holiday decorations to the ownership of shared amenities. Residents found themselves entangled in a web of rules and regulations, subject to the whims of unelected boards and committees.

As we journey through the early days of HOAs, we uncover the tensions simmering beneath the surface—tensions that would eventually erupt into full-blown conflicts between homeowners seeking to assert their rights and HOAs clinging to their authority. It is a story of idealism and disillusionment, of promises made and broken, and of the unintended consequences of well-intentioned planning.

AN IMAGE OF EARLY HOMESTEADING IN AMERICA

In the vast expanse of the American frontier, a pioneering spirit thrived—a spirit of self-reliance, resilience, and the pursuit of a better life. This chapter transports us back to the formative years of homesteading in America, a time when the promise of land and opportunity beckoned settlers westward and the dream of building a home from scratch fueled the imagination of generations.

The story of homesteading is intertwined with the very fabric of American history, stretching back to the Homestead Act of 1862—a landmark piece of legislation that offered 160 acres of free land to settlers willing to cultivate and improve it. This bold initiative, signed into law by President Abraham Lincoln, was a catalyst for westward expansion and the settlement of vast tracts of land previously inhabited by indigenous peoples.

With Ralph Waldo Emerson and Henry David Thoreau, who championed the virtues of simplicity, harmony with nature, and agrarian living, we can paint a vivid picture of homesteading during the early days of America's history. We can picture a true spirit of autonomy. Where people began to journey out onto their own. People started moving away from the thirteen colonies and settled West in an effort to make a name for their selves which in that day in age meant eating well. We can picture a sense of where the birthplace of preservation and conservation began. With scenes from these two characters, I believe that this is where redirection for global warming began and this is where its inspiration stems from. That is; the cure for global warming being the respect and upmost integrity for nature and being one with the land.

People during this time really thrived with community as they were truly a team. They hunted game, traded goods with neighboring settlers, and formed tight-knit communities bound by shared struggles and triumphs. They had celebrations together they did harvests together and shared implementation and trade secrets with each other in a boundless bounty of their great earth at the time.

You truly couldn't do it without a community in those days. It truly did take a village to raise your kids like Aristotle said in a famous quote. It was a team effort. Think of a whole neighborhood in this day in age getting together to have a small school or getting together to do a village sick clinic where doctors roamed from house to house and were on call meaning that whoever was within earshot were their only clients.

Wendell Berry describes in his historical fiction series called Port Williams where homesteading communities similar to the Zen of Henry David Thoreau lived beautifully and at one with their surrounding in a peaceful elegant way. Wendell Berry is known for different studies himself being greatly related to global warming and the effect of the two of his books have on the reader is a time where global warming was at a standstill, and there was little that we were doing to the land that was not evil. This was a time, just like in his novels where people having small outcroppings of farms on just about every property, and there was not what there is now with big giant fields as far as you can see. There just was no application for that. It was still plowed by the animals and it just wasn't feasible to do big crop fields. Instead they were very diverse farms, which is what they are teaching now with global warming is what we need to get back to. They had diverse farms witch lead to rich soil and in turn a healthier environment.

In the vast expanse of the American frontier, a pioneering spirit thrived—a spirit of self-reliance, resilience, and the pursuit of a better life. This chapter transports us back to the formative years of homesteading in America, a time when the promise of land and opportunity beckoned settlers westward and the dream of building a home from scratch fueled the imagination of generations.

The story of homesteading is intertwined with the very fabric of American history, stretching back to the Homestead Act of 1862—a landmark piece of legislation that offered 160 acres of free land to settlers willing to cultivate and improve it. This bold initiative, signed into law by President Abraham Lincoln, was a catalyst for westward expansion and the settlement of vast tracts of land previously inhabited by indigenous peoples.

With figures like Ralph Waldo Emerson and Henry David Thoreau championing the virtues of simplicity, harmony with nature, and agrarian living, we can paint a vivid picture of homesteading during the early days of America's history. It was a time of true autonomy, where individuals embarked on journeys to establish their own homesteads, seeking sustenance and prosperity from the land.

Communities formed organically, with settlers relying on one another for survival. They hunted game, traded goods with neighboring homesteaders, and celebrated together. Wendell Berry's historical fiction series, such as Port Williams, beautifully captures the essence of these homesteading communities, where individuals lived in harmony with their surroundings, tending to diverse farms and fostering a deep connection to the land.

During this era, the concept of community was paramount. As Aristotle famously said, "It takes a village to raise a child." Settlers relied on each other for support, sharing knowledge and resources in a collective effort to thrive in their new environment. Medical care, education, and other necessities were often communal endeavors, reflecting the interdependence of frontier life.

The practices of early homesteaders, characterized by diversity in farming and a reverence for nature, offer valuable lessons for addressing modern challenges like global warming. By returning to a model of small-scale, diverse agriculture, we can nurture healthier environments and communities, echoing the sustainable practices of our forebears on the American frontier.

03

THE DYNAMICS OF COMMUNITY GOVERNANCE

In this chapter, we delve into the intricate evolution of community governance, tracing its trajectory from the grassroots initiatives of early settlements to the complexities of modern homeowners associations (HOAs). Through the lens of history, law, and social dynamics, we explore the shifting tides of collective organization and individual autonomy.

From homesteading to municipalities, we embark on a journey back to the formative years of American settlement, where pioneering spirits established homesteads and formed tight-knit communities based on mutual aid and cooperation. With the expansion of urban centers came the rise of municipalities, marking a transition from informal community governance to structured systems of local government.

Navigating Regulatory Landscapes is and was a tough thing as far as HOAs are concerned. As cities grew and land use became more regulated, zoning laws and ordinances emerged to manage urban development and ensure public welfare. We examine the tensions between government oversight and individual freedoms, as communities grappled with questions of property rights, community aesthetics, and the common good.

The Emergence of HOAs took quite a short amount of time. Against the backdrop of municipal governance, the modern homeowners association (HOA) emerged as a private alternative, offering residents greater control over neighborhood aesthetics and amenities. We delve into the motivations behind the rise of HOAs and the promises of communal harmony and increased property values that they offered to homeowners.

However, the implementation of HOAs also brought forth a host of challenges and controversies. Disputes over rule enforcement, fee structures, and governance processes strained the relationship between HOAs and homeowners, revealing deeper tensions surrounding individual rights and collective responsibilities.

Legal and Legislative Responses were an integral part of the start up of the HOA In response to mounting criticism and legal battles, lawmakers intervened to regulate HOA operations and protect homeowners' rights. State statutes and legal precedents reshaped the legal landscape, establishing frameworks to address governance issues and ensure transparency and accountability within HOA communities.

Recognizing the need for collaborative approaches, stakeholders from diverse backgrounds worked together to promote dialogue, foster inclusivity, and empower residents within HOA communities. Through community engagement and advocacy efforts, they sought to reconcile competing interests and forge stronger, more resilient communities for the future.

As we journey through the complexities of community governance, we uncover the delicate balance between collective interests and individual liberties. From the humble beginnings of homesteading to the intricacies of modern HOAs, the quest for equitable, participatory governance remains an ongoing endeavor—one that requires ongoing dialogue, collaboration, and a commitment to the common good.

In this chapter, we delve into the intricate evolution of community governance, tracing its trajectory from the grassroots initiatives of early settlements to the complexities of modern homeowners associations (HOAs). Through the lens of history, law, and social dynamics, we explore the shifting tides of collective organization and individual autonomy.

From Homesteading to Municipalities, We embark on a journey back to the formative years of American settlement, where pioneering spirits established homesteads and formed tight-knit communities based on mutual aid and cooperation. With the expansion of urban centers came the rise of municipalities, marking a transition from informal community governance to structured systems of local government.

Navigating Regulatory Landscapes was big during the years of the birthplace of HOAs. As cities grew and land use became more regulated, zoning laws and ordinances emerged to manage urban development and ensure public welfare. We examine the tensions between government oversight and individual freedoms, as communities grappled with questions of property rights, community aesthetics, and the common good.

The Emergence of HOAs was a unique time. Against the backdrop of municipal governance, the modern homeowners association (HOA) emerged as a private alternative, offering residents greater control over neighborhood aesthetics and amenities. We delve into the motivations behind the rise of HOAs and the promises of communal harmony and increased property values that they offered to homeowners.

However, the implementation of HOAs also brought forth a host of challenges and controversies. Disputes over rule enforcement, fee structures, and governance processes strained the relationship between HOAs and homeowners, revealing deeper tensions surrounding individual rights and collective responsibilities.

Legal and Legislative Responses were present during the time of HOAs. In response to mounting criticism and legal battles, lawmakers intervened to regulate HOA operations and protect homeowners' rights. State statutes and legal precedents reshaped the legal landscape, establishing frameworks to address governance issues and ensure transparency and accountability within HOA communities.

Toward Collaborative Solutions, Recognizing the need for collaborative approaches, stakeholders from diverse backgrounds worked together to promote dialogue, foster inclusivity, and empower residents within HOA communities. Through community engagement and advocacy efforts, they sought to reconcile competing interests and forge stronger, more resilient communities for the future.

As we journey through the complexities of community governance, we uncover the delicate balance between collective interests and individual liberties. From the humble beginnings of homesteading to the intricacies of modern HOAs, the quest for equitable, participatory governance remains an ongoing endeavor—one that requires ongoing dialogue, collaboration, and a commitment to the common good.

CHAPTER

04

THE ENVIRONMENTAL FALLOUT OF HOAS AND INDUSTRIAL AGRICULTURE

As the suburban landscape flourished under the reign of homeowners associations (HOAs), another less visible but equally impactful transformation was underway: the industrialization of agriculture. This chapter delves into the environmental repercussions of both phenomena and their intertwined consequences for global warming and community resilience.

Mono-cropping and Soil Degradation were something that happened because of the explosion of population. With the rise of industrial agriculture came the widespread adoption of mono-cropping, a practice that prioritizes high-yield, single-crop cultivation over diverse farming methods. While mono-cropping maximized efficiency and output, it also depleted soil nutrients, eroded topsoil, and disrupted natural ecosystems. As a result, soil health deteriorated, leading to decreased agricultural productivity and increased vulnerability to erosion, drought, and pest infestations.

Soil Testing and Agricultural Policies were a big part of the change. The implementation of soil testing in industrial agriculture further exacerbated environmental degradation and land consolidation. As mono-cropping depleted soil fertility, farmers relied heavily on synthetic fertilizers to maintain productivity. However, indiscriminate fertilizer application led to nutrient runoff, water pollution, and soil acidification, further degrading soil quality and ecosystem health. Moreover, agricultural policies incentivized monoculture and large-scale farming operations, consolidating land ownership and displacing small-scale farmers and rural communities.

The Tyranny of Agribusiness Tycoons were similar to that of the HOA. As industrial agriculture gained dominance, agribusiness tycoons capitalized on land consolidation and monopolized food production, distribution, and supply chains. Through lobbying, market manipulation, and predatory practices, these corporate giants wielded immense influence over agricultural policies, shaping regulatory frameworks to favor their interests at the expense of environmental sustainability, food sovereignty, and community resilience. Consequently, small farmers were marginalized, rural economies were destabilized, and biodiversity was threatened, exacerbating social inequalities and ecological vulnerabilities.

The HOAs and Agricultural land conversion both seemed similar in that they both were tycoon-owned and both were an effort to grab up land and make money off it. Meanwhile, the proliferation of HOAs facilitated urban sprawl and encroachment into agricultural lands, accelerating land conversion and habitat loss. As suburban communities expanded, prime farmland was transformed into residential developments, shopping centers, and infrastructure projects, fragmenting landscapes, depleting natural resources, and diminishing biodiversity. This land-use change further compounded environmental degradation, exacerbating climate change, and undermining community resilience.

The Vicious Cycle of Consumerism and Environmental Degradation were a big part of both of these in history. In the nexus of HOAs, industrial agriculture, and consumer culture, a vicious cycle of environmental degradation was perpetuated. As suburban lifestyles embraced convenience, consumption, and conformity, demand for industrially produced food, goods, and services skyrocketed, driving resource extraction, pollution, and waste generation. This insatiable appetite for growth and consumption fueled a feedback loop of environmental degradation, exacerbating global warming, biodiversity loss, and social inequities.

Breaking the Chains of Unsustainable Practices became the focus point over the next piece of history. In the face of mounting environmental challenges, the imperative to break free from unsustainable practices has never been more urgent. From regenerative agriculture and community-supported agriculture (CSA) initiatives to sustainable land-use planning and grassroots activism, there exists a myriad of pathways toward resilience, sustainability, and community empowerment. By reimagining our relationship with the land, embracing diversity, and reclaiming local food systems, we can cultivate a more equitable, resilient, and regenerative future for all.

As the suburban landscape flourished under the reign of homeowners associations (HOAs), another less visible but equally impactful transformation was underway: the industrialization of agriculture. This chapter delves into the environmental repercussions of both phenomena and their intertwined consequences for global warming and community resilience.

Mono-cropping and Soil Degradation led to the Dust Bowl. With the rise of industrial agriculture came the widespread adoption of mono-cropping, a practice that prioritizes high-yield, single-crop cultivation over diverse farming methods. While mono-cropping maximized efficiency and output, it also depleted soil nutrients, eroded topsoil, and disrupted natural ecosystems. As a result, soil health deteriorated, leading to decreased agricultural productivity and increased vulnerability to erosion, drought, and pest infestations.

The implementation of soil testing in industrial agriculture further exacerbated environmental degradation and land consolidation. As mono-cropping depleted soil fertility, farmers relied heavily on synthetic fertilizers to maintain productivity. However, indiscriminate fertilizer application led to nutrient runoff, water pollution, and soil acidification, further degrading soil quality and ecosystem health. Moreover, agricultural policies incentivized monoculture and large-scale farming operations, consolidating land ownership and displacing small-scale farmers and rural communities.

The Tyranny of Agribusiness Tycoons were prevalent during this time. As industrial agriculture gained dominance, agribusiness tycoons capitalized on land consolidation and monopolized food production, distribution, and supply chains. Through lobbying, market manipulation, and predatory practices, these corporate giants wielded immense influence over agricultural policies, shaping regulatory frameworks to favor their interests at the expense of environmental sustainability, food sovereignty, and community resilience. Consequently, small farmers were marginalized, rural economies were destabilized, and biodiversity was threatened, exacerbating social inequalities and ecological vulnerabilities.

HOAs and Agricultural Land Conversion happened at about the same time. Meanwhile, the proliferation of HOAs facilitated urban sprawl and encroachment into agricultural lands, accelerating land conversion and habitat loss. As suburban communities expanded, prime farmland was transformed into residential developments, shopping centers, and infrastructure projects, fragmenting landscapes, depleting natural resources, and diminishing biodiversity. This land-use change further compounded environmental degradation, exacerbating climate change, and undermining community resilience.

The Vicious Cycle of Consumerism and Environmental Degradation is a big deal. In the nexus of HOAs, industrial agriculture, and consumer culture, a vicious cycle of environmental degradation was perpetuated. As suburban lifestyles embraced convenience, consumption, and conformity, demand for industrially produced food, goods, and services skyrocketed, driving resource extraction, pollution, and waste generation. This insatiable appetite for growth and consumption fueled a feedback loop of environmental degradation, exacerbating global warming, biodiversity loss, and social inequities.

Breaking the Chains of Unsustainable Practices is a necessity. In the face of mounting environmental challenges, the imperative to break free from unsustainable practices has never been more urgent. From regenerative agriculture and community-supported agriculture (CSA) initiatives to sustainable land-use planning and grassroots activism, there exists a myriad of pathways toward resilience, sustainability, and community empowerment. By reimagining our relationship with the land, embracing diversity, and reclaiming local food systems, we can cultivate a more equitable, resilient, and regenerative future for all.

CHAPTER

05

THE UNRAVELING OF
HOA HEGEMONY

As the allure of suburban utopia promised by homeowners associations (HOAs) began to fade, cracks in the foundation of their governance model widened, revealing deeper fissures in community cohesion and individual rights. This chapter examines the unraveling of HOA hegemony and the emergence of grassroots resistance movements seeking to reclaim autonomy and restore community democracy.

Erosion of Trust and Transparency Over time, residents within HOA communities grew disillusioned with opaque decision-making processes, arbitrary rule enforcement, and escalating fee structures. Trust between homeowners and HOA boards eroded as conflicts over governance, finances, and accountability escalated, undermining the very essence of community cohesion and shared responsibility. Rise of Homeowner Advocacy Groups Faced with mounting grievances and a sense of powerlessness, homeowners began to organize grassroots advocacy groups to challenge HOA authority and demand greater transparency, accountability, and resident participation. These movements, fueled by a desire for democratic governance and individual liberties, sought to rebalance the scales of power and restore community autonomy. Legal Battles and Legislative Reforms As homeowner advocacy groups gained momentum, legal battles erupted over property rights, due process, and constitutional protections within HOA communities. Landmark court cases and legislative reforms reshaped the legal landscape, affirming homeowners' rights to challenge HOA decisions, access records, and participate in governance processes. State lawmakers enacted statutes to curb HOA abuses and protect residents from arbitrary rule enforcement and financial mismanagement.

Recognizing the limitations of traditional HOA structures, stakeholders explored alternative governance models rooted in participatory democracy, consensus-building, and community empowerment. From cooperative housing associations to cohousing communities and intentional neighborhoods, residents embraced collaborative approaches to decision-making, conflict resolution, and resource sharing, fostering a sense of belonging, reciprocity, and collective responsibility.

With the advent of digital technologies and online platforms, communities transcended physical boundaries, enabling virtual engagement, knowledge sharing, and collective action. Online forums, social media groups, and digital tools empowered residents to connect, collaborate, and mobilize around shared interests and concerns, amplifying their voices and fostering a sense of belonging in an increasingly fragmented world.

As the unraveling of HOA hegemony unfolds, a new paradigm of community governance emerges—one rooted in transparency, accountability, and resident empowerment. By embracing principles of equity, inclusion, and participatory democracy, communities can navigate complexity, build resilience, and foster vibrant, thriving neighborhoods that reflect the diverse needs, aspirations, and values of their residents.

In the aftermath of the rise and ruin of HOAs, communities stand at a crossroads, poised to chart a new course toward a more just, sustainable, and equitable future. By harnessing the collective wisdom, creativity, and resilience of their residents, communities can forge pathways of renewal, regeneration, and shared prosperity for generations to come.

As the allure of suburban utopia promised by homeowners associations (HOAs) began to fade, cracks in the foundation of their governance model widened, revealing deeper fissures in community cohesion and individual rights. This chapter examines the unraveling of HOA hegemony and the emergence of grassroots resistance movements seeking to reclaim autonomy and restore community democracy.

Over time, residents within HOA communities grew disillusioned with opaque decision-making processes, arbitrary rule enforcement, and escalating fee structures. Trust between homeowners and HOA boards eroded as conflicts over governance, finances, and accountability escalated, undermining the very essence of community cohesion and shared responsibility.

Faced with mounting grievances and a sense of powerlessness, homeowners began to organize grassroots advocacy groups to challenge HOA authority and demand greater transparency, accountability, and resident participation. These movements, fueled by a desire for democratic governance and individual liberties, sought to rebalance the scales of power and restore community autonomy.

As homeowner advocacy groups gained momentum, legal battles erupted over property rights, due process, and constitutional protections within HOA communities. Landmark court cases and legislative reforms reshaped the legal landscape, affirming homeowners' rights to challenge HOA decisions, access records, and participate in governance processes.

State lawmakers enacted statutes to curb HOA abuses and protect residents from arbitrary rule enforcement and financial mismanagement.

Recognizing the limitations of traditional HOA structures, stakeholders explored alternative governance models rooted in participatory democracy, consensus-building, and community empowerment. From cooperative housing associations to cohousing communities and intentional neighborhoods, residents embraced collaborative approaches to decision-making, conflict resolution, and resource sharing, fostering a sense of belonging, reciprocity, and collective responsibility.

With the advent of digital technologies and online platforms, communities transcended physical boundaries, enabling virtual engagement, knowledge sharing, and collective action. Online forums, social media groups, and digital tools empowered residents to connect, collaborate, and mobilize around shared interests and concerns, amplifying their voices and fostering a sense of belonging in an increasingly fragmented world.

As the unraveling of HOA hegemony unfolds, a new paradigm of community governance emerges—one rooted in transparency, accountability, and resident empowerment. By embracing principles of equity, inclusion, and participatory democracy, communities can navigate complexity, build resilience, and foster vibrant, thriving neighborhoods that reflect the diverse needs, aspirations, and values of their residents.

In the aftermath of the rise and ruin of HOAs, communities stand at a crossroads, poised to chart a new course toward a more just, sustainable, and equitable future. By harnessing the collective wisdom, creativity, and resilience of their residents, communities can forge pathways of renewal, regeneration, and shared prosperity for generations to come.

CHAPTER

06

THE ANTAGONIST RULES
OF THE HOA

Some of the rules seem outdated and erroneous. Every cooking cutter house within the HOA now seems to be a mold of the past and not something that is needed or wanted anymore.

With global warming it seems like neighborhoods need to move back to homesteading and not towards more rules and regulations in order for the big man behind the money to benefit.

Too long has it been the real estate tycoons jobs to rack up the prices of conjoined houses. Now it is the little guy's turn make a difference and own what he has and let the inspiration of homesteading prevail.

Some rules are different with different counties and it kind of depends where you are at to decide which rule pertains to which area. Like in my folks area there is a restriction that a code enforcement has jurisdiction over that states that homeowners cannot even have bees.

Not only is this a tragedy but this is a big deal for pollenators. Whereas in Boulder the county right next door bees take precedence and are on the forefront of peoples minds and rules. Boulder is a more lienient community as far as chickens go too. I think it is the same law that enforces the right over the county's law vs the HOAs rules that presides.

In some counties it depends within the general location of the house and you have to get a certain permit or license to keep bees or chickens or any other livestock or agriculture. That is you must be in a regulated zone and it must be free from county rules as well as the coded area as well as the HOA zone.

As communities evolve and societal values shift, the once well-intentioned rules and regulations of homeowners associations (HOAs) often find themselves outdated and out of touch with the needs and desires of residents. In this chapter, we confront the antagonist rules that have become emblematic of HOA governance, exploring their origins, impact, and the growing resistance against their hegemony.

Within many HOAs, a sense of uniformity and conformity prevails, with cookie-cutter houses and rigid aesthetic standards dominating the landscape. Yet, as societal attitudes toward diversity, sustainability, and individual expression evolve, these once-cherished ideals of homogeneity have come under scrutiny. Residents increasingly push back against outdated regulations that stifle creativity, limit personalization, and fail to reflect the diverse identities and lifestyles within their communities.

In the face of mounting environmental challenges, the principles of homesteading—self-reliance, sustainability, and harmony with nature—offer an alternative vision to the restrictive dictates of HOAs. While HOAs prioritize uniformity and centralized control, homesteading celebrates diversity, autonomy, and community resilience. As the urgency of climate change compels communities to rethink their relationship with the land, the ethos of homesteading emerges as a potent antidote to the hegemony of HOAs and the industrialization of agriculture.

The jurisdictional patchwork of rules and regulations further complicates matters for residents seeking to exercise their rights within HOA communities. Varying county ordinances, municipal codes, and HOA bylaws create confusion and inconsistency, leaving homeowners unsure of which rules apply and how to navigate conflicting mandates. The need for clarity, transparency, and alignment between different regulatory frameworks becomes increasingly apparent as residents seek to assert their autonomy and reclaim control over their properties.

Despite the challenges posed by HOA regulations, residents are mobilizing to challenge the status quo and reclaim their rights within their communities. Grassroots advocacy groups, legal challenges, and legislative reforms are empowering homeowners to push back against arbitrary rule enforcement, excessive fees, and lack of accountability within HOA governance structures. By amplifying their voices and mobilizing collective action, residents are asserting their agency and reshaping the dynamics of community governance from within.

As communities grapple with the legacy of HOA hegemony and the complexities of modern governance, a paradigm shift is underway—one that prioritizes equity, inclusivity, and resident empowerment. By embracing principles of participatory democracy, environmental stewardship, and cultural diversity, communities can chart a new course toward a more just, sustainable, and equitable future. Through dialogue, collaboration, and collective action, residents can reimagine the role of HOAs as facilitators of community well-being and guardians of shared prosperity.

In the face of mounting environmental challenges and evolving societal norms, the antagonistic rules of HOAs stand as a relic of a bygone era. Yet, as residents assert their rights and reclaim their autonomy, the seeds of change are sown, paving the way for a more inclusive, resilient, and vibrant future for HOA communities and beyond.

As communities evolve and societal values shift, the once well-intentioned rules and regulations of homeowners associations (HOAs) often find themselves outdated and out of touch with the needs and desires of residents. In this chapter, we confront the antagonist rules that have become emblematic of HOA governance, exploring their origins, impact, and the growing resistance against their hegemony.

Outdated Regulations and Cookie-Cutter Homes are a thing of the past but still come up in recent books. Within many HOAs, a sense of uniformity and conformity prevails, with cookie-cutter houses and rigid aesthetic standards dominating the landscape. Yet, as societal attitudes toward diversity, sustainability, and individual expression evolve, these once-cherished ideals of homogeneity have come under scrutiny. Residents increasingly push back against outdated regulations that stifle creativity, limit personalization, and fail to reflect the diverse identities and lifestyles within their communities.

In the face of mounting environmental challenges, the principles of homesteading—self-reliance, sustainability, and harmony with nature—offer an alternative vision to the restrictive dictates of HOAs. While HOAs prioritize uniformity and centralized control, homesteading celebrates diversity, autonomy, and community resilience. As the urgency of climate change compels communities to rethink their relationship with the land, the ethos of homesteading emerges as a potent antidote to the hegemony of HOAs and the industrialization of agriculture.

The jurisdictional patchwork of rules and regulations further complicates matters for residents seeking to exercise their rights within HOA communities. Varying county ordinances, municipal codes, and HOA bylaws create confusion and inconsistency, leaving homeowners unsure of which rules apply and how to navigate conflicting mandates. The need for clarity, transparency, and alignment between different regulatory frameworks becomes increasingly apparent as residents seek to assert their autonomy and reclaim control over their properties.

Despite the challenges posed by HOA regulations, residents are mobilizing to challenge the status quo and reclaim their rights within their communities. Grassroots advocacy groups, legal challenges, and legislative reforms are empowering homeowners to push back against arbitrary rule enforcement, excessive fees, and lack of accountability within HOA governance structures. By amplifying their voices and mobilizing collective action, residents are asserting their agency and reshaping the dynamics of community governance from within.

As communities grapple with the legacy of HOA hegemony and the complexities of modern governance, a paradigm shift is underway—one that prioritizes equity, inclusivity, and resident empowerment. By embracing principles of participatory democracy, environmental stewardship, and cultural diversity, communities can chart a new course toward a more just, sustainable, and equitable future. Through dialogue, collaboration, and collective action, residents can reimagine the role of HOAs as facilitators of community well-being and guardians of shared prosperity.

In the face of mounting environmental challenges and evolving societal norms, the antagonistic rules of HOAs stand as a relic of a bygone era. Yet, as residents assert their rights and reclaim their autonomy, the seeds of change are sown, paving the way for a more inclusive, resilient, and vibrant future for HOA communities and beyond.

07

ZEROSCAPING AND WATER DISPLACEMENT

During the HOAs demise which is right now in this point in history some areas like for homeowners to have a certain type of grass and a certain length, and most require that you cut your grass. While this may look good for global warming in that every person has their own photosynthesis patchwork right in front of their house, it is not good because of the general size of the population.

With overpopulation water displacement is a huge factor in the survival of our species. There have been a number of govenors including Jared Polis in our state that wrote policy giving incentive to homeowners to go for zeroscaping. Which is a landscaping value that only uses plants from the local and surrounding ecosystem to integrate into your house aesthetics. Rooted in principles of water efficiency, native plant selection, and soil conservation, xeriscaping offers homeowners a pathway to reduce water consumption, minimize maintenance, and enhance ecological resilience in their outdoor spaces. By embracing drought-tolerant plants, mulch, and efficient irrigation systems, residents can create vibrant, water-wise landscapes that thrive in harmony with local ecosystems.

When thinking about water and where it is put, we don't want to put it just onto something that looks good and has no purpose. It is getting so scare and will become an endangered resource so fast that it needs to have a purpose. And a good one at that. During times of drought we have seen that policy makers make it mandatory that our water be shut off first of all on our lawns and that we only use certain amounts for our washing machine and for showers throughout the day.

This is a huge factor when thinking about global warming. We already have a population problem and it would just add to the panic when people run out of water in a drought situation. This you could imagine would be horrible.

Think of all the lawns that are going to need new implementation as well. If we do make the change to just electric instead of curbing the water displacement issue, then we will need an electric lawn mower and instruments like weed trimmers and hedgetrimmers along with that as well for ever person that resides in an HOA. That is a lot of people and a lot of equipment.

As water scarcity becomes an increasingly pressing concern, policymakers and water utilities are implementing mandates and incentives to promote water conservation at the community level. HOAs are encouraged to adopt xeriscaping guidelines, enforce water-efficient landscaping practices, and incentivize residents to minimize outdoor water usage through rebates, education, and outreach efforts. By prioritizing water conservation measures, HOAs can play a pivotal role in mitigating the impacts of drought, preserving natural resources, and promoting community resilience.

It could be argued that the water displacement problem especially with droughts and the fear of overpopulation have the ability to be as big a problem as soil conservation was back in the industrial revolution. However, with education, outreach, and collaborative engagement, communities can overcome barriers to change and embrace sustainable land-scaping as a shared value and collective responsibility. This is how the soil was restored and knowledge about soil integrity and diversity was spread around the community.

As water scarcity becomes an increasingly pressing concern, policymakers and water utilities are implementing mandates and incentives to promote water conservation at the community level. HOAs are encouraged to adopt xeriscaping guidelines, enforce water-efficient landscaping practices, and incentivize residents to minimize outdoor water usage through rebates, education, and outreach efforts. By prioritizing water conservation measures, HOAs can play a pivotal role in mitigating the impacts of drought, preserving natural resources, and promoting community resilience.

It could be argued that the water displacement problem, especially during droughts and concerns about overpopulation, has the potential to be as significant an issue as soil conservation was during the Industrial Revolution. However, with education, outreach, and collaborative engagement, communities can overcome barriers to change and embrace sustainable landscaping as a shared value and collective responsibility. This parallels the historical efforts to restore soil integrity and promote diversity within communities.

As HOAs navigate the challenges of water scarcity and overpopulation, they have an opportunity to lead by example and inspire residents to adopt practices that prioritize water efficiency, native plant selection, and ecological resilience. By fostering a culture of environmental stewardship and collective action, HOAs can contribute to a more sustainable future for their communities and beyond.

CHAPTER

08

GOLF COARSES

Golf courses have long been emblematic of suburban living, offering lush green landscapes and recreational opportunities for residents within homeowners associations (HOAs). However, as communities grapple with the environmental consequences of land use and water consumption, the role of golf courses has come under scrutiny. In this chapter, we explore the tensions surrounding golf courses within HOA communities and their impact on water resources, biodiversity, and community well-being.

Golf courses are notorious for their high water consumption, chemical inputs, and habitat disruption. The vast expanses of manicured turf require intensive irrigation to maintain their aesthetic appeal, placing significant strain on local water supplies, particularly in arid regions. Moreover, the use of pesticides, herbicides, and fertilizers poses risks to wildlife, soil health, and water quality, contributing to ecological degradation and biodiversity loss.

The reliance on irrigation for golf course maintenance exacerbates water scarcity concerns, especially in regions facing drought conditions. As water resources become increasingly scarce and valuable, communities must confront the trade-offs between recreational amenities and water conservation. Efforts to improve water efficiency, adopt drought-tolerant landscaping, and implement alternative irrigation strategies can help mitigate the environmental impacts of golf courses while ensuring sustainable water management practices.

Golf courses have the potential to serve as refuges for wildlife and contribute to ecological diversity when managed with conservation principles in mind. By incorporating native vegetation, wetlands, and wildlife corridors into course design, golf courses can provide habitat for a variety of plant and animal species, enhance ecosystem resilience, and promote environmental stewardship within HOA communities. However, the indiscriminate use of pesticides and habitat fragmentation pose significant threats to biodiversity and ecosystem health, underscoring the need for proactive conservation measures.

The future of golf courses within HOA communities hinges on collaborative engagement, environmental stewardship, and sustainable management practices. Residents, HOA boards, and golf course operators must work together to strike a balance between recreational enjoyment and environmental responsibility. Through education, outreach, and innovative approaches to course design and maintenance, communities can transform golf courses into models of sustainable land use, conservation, and community well-being.

Golf courses had to be a subject when talking about water displacement and HOAs because they are a big part of both. In the era of global warming, the conversation surrounding golf courses within HOA communities extends beyond recreation to encompass broader environmental and social considerations. With both considered we need to be weary of how we have built them in the past in order to have a good idea of how harmful they have been to our society. With golf courses and some HOAs we have sought land that was needed to be used for natural ecosystems. We bought this land that was designated for conservation and used it in a sense that is quoted as being natural, but has been a destructive force non the less. We must brace for this in the future and make big changes within the sport of golf and with purchasing up more land for the use of both of these concepts.

Golf courses have long been emblematic of suburban living, offering lush green landscapes and recreational opportunities for residents within homeowners associations (HOAs). However, as communities grapple with the environmental consequences of land use and water consumption, the role of golf courses has come under scrutiny. In this chapter, we explore the tensions surrounding golf courses within HOA communities and their impact on water resources, biodiversity, and community well-being.

Golf courses are notorious for their high water consumption, chemical inputs, and habitat disruption. The vast expanses of manicured turf require intensive irrigation to maintain their aesthetic appeal, placing significant strain on local water supplies, particularly in arid regions. Moreover, the use of pesticides, herbicides, and fertilizers poses risks to wildlife, soil health, and water quality, contributing to ecological degradation and biodiversity loss.

The reliance on irrigation for golf course maintenance exacerbates water scarcity concerns, especially in regions facing drought conditions. As water resources become increasingly scarce and valuable, communities must confront the trade-offs between recreational amenities and water conservation. Efforts to improve water efficiency, adopt drought-tolerant landscaping, and implement alternative irrigation strategies can help mitigate the environmental impacts of golf courses while ensuring sustainable water management practices.

Golf courses have the potential to serve as refuges for wildlife and contribute to ecological diversity when managed with conservation principles in mind. By incorporating native vegetation, wetlands, and wildlife corridors into course design, golf courses can provide habitat for a variety of plant and animal species, enhance ecosystem resilience, and promote environmental stewardship within HOA communities. However, the indiscriminate use of pesticides and habitat fragmentation pose significant threats to biodiversity and ecosystem health, underscoring the need for proactive conservation measures.

The future of golf courses within HOA communities hinges on collaborative engagement, environmental stewardship, and sustainable management practices. Residents, HOA boards, and golf course operators must work together to strike a balance between recreational enjoyment and environmental responsibility. Through education, outreach, and innovative approaches to course design and maintenance, communities can transform golf courses into models of sustainable land use, conservation, and community well-being.

In the era of global warming, the conversation surrounding golf courses within HOA communities extends beyond recreation to encompass broader environmental and social considerations. With both considered, we need to be wary of how we have built them in the past in order to have a good idea of how harmful they have been to our society. With golf courses and some HOAs, we have sought land that was needed to be used for natural ecosystems. We bought this land that was designated for conservation and used it in a sense that is quoted as being natural but has been a destructive force nonetheless. We must brace for this in the future and make significant changes within the sport of golf and with purchasing up more land for the use of both of these concepts.

Chapter: Ski Town HOAs

In a ski town HOA, the dynamics of community living and property management are uniquely shaped by the seasonal nature of the area's primary industry and the recreational lifestyle it promotes. As residents and property owners come together to navigate the challenges and opportunities of living in a ski town, the role of the HOA becomes particularly significant in ensuring the well-being of the community and the effective management of shared resources.

1. **Seasonal Fluctuations and Tourism:** One of the defining features of a ski town HOA is the seasonal fluctuations in population and tourism. During peak ski season, the town experiences an influx of visitors and second-home owners, leading to increased demand for services and amenities. The HOA plays a crucial role in coordinating these efforts, from snow removal and shuttle services to maintaining common areas and facilities. Additionally, the HOA may implement seasonal

regulations or restrictions to manage noise, parking, and other issues associated with increased activity.

2. **Recreational Amenities:** Ski town HOAs often prioritize access to recreational amenities such as ski slopes, hiking trails, and fitness centers. These amenities not only enhance the quality of life for residents but also attract visitors and potential buyers. The HOA may be responsible for managing and maintaining these facilities, including scheduling maintenance, hiring staff, and enforcing usage rules. Furthermore, the HOA may collaborate with local businesses and organizations to offer discounts or promotions for residents and guests.

3. **Environmental Stewardship:** Ski towns are typically situated in environmentally sensitive areas, surrounded by forests, mountains, and waterways. The HOA plays a critical role in promoting environmental stewardship and sustainable practices within the community. This may include implementing recycling programs, conserving water and energy, and preserving natural habitats. Additionally, the HOA may partner with local conservation groups or government agencies to address issues such as wildfire prevention, wildlife management, and trail maintenance.

4. **Short-Term Rentals and Property Management:** With the rise of short-term rental platforms like Airbnb and VRBO, ski town HOAs face unique challenges related to property management and community cohesion. The HOA may establish regulations or guidelines governing short-term rentals, including occupancy limits, noise restrictions, and parking policies. Additionally, the HOA may provide resources or assistance to homeowners managing rental properties, such as property management services or educational workshops.

5. **Community Engagement and Events:** Ski town HOAs often host community events and activities to foster a sense of belonging and camaraderie among residents. These may include holiday celebrations, social gatherings, and outdoor festivals. The HOA plays a central role in organizing and promoting these events, as well as providing support and resources to community members who wish to organize their own activities. Furthermore, the HOA may facilitate communication and collaboration among residents through newsletters, social media, and online forums.

6. **Financial Management and Budgeting:** Effective financial management is essential for the long-term sustainability of a ski town HOA. The HOA is responsible for collecting dues and assessments from homeowners, as well as budgeting and allocating funds for maintenance, repairs, and capital improvements. Additionally, the HOA may establish reserve funds for future projects or emergencies and work with financial advisors or accountants to ensure fiscal responsibility and transparency.

In summary, a ski town HOA plays a multifaceted role in managing the unique challenges and opportunities of living in a recreational destination. By promoting community engagement, environmental stewardship, and effective property management, the HOA helps to create a vibrant and sustainable community where residents and visitors alike can thrive.

Chapter: The Environmental Impact of Ski Town HOAs: Assessing Their Role in Global Warming

While ski town homeowners associations (HOAs) often serve as pillars of community governance and management, their operations and policies can have significant implications for the environment, particularly in the context of global warming. Despite the allure of picturesque mountain landscapes and world-class recreational opportunities, the environmental footprint of ski resorts and their associated HOAs warrants careful examination. Let's delve into why ski town HOAs might contribute to global warming, depending on the specific characteristics and practices of the ski resort.

1. **Energy Consumption:** Ski resorts require substantial amounts of energy to operate lifts, snowmaking equipment, and facilities such as lodges, restaurants, and rental shops. The HOA may oversee the management and maintenance of these facilities, making decisions about energy sources, efficiency upgrades, and conservation measures. In some cases, ski town HOAs may rely heavily on fossil fuels for energy generation, contributing to greenhouse gas emissions and exacerbating global warming. Additionally, the energy-intensive nature of snowmaking can further strain local resources and ecosystems, particularly in water-stressed regions.

2. **Transportation Emissions:** Ski resorts often attract visitors from far and wide, leading to increased transportation emissions associated with travel to and from the resort. While the HOA may implement shuttle services, carpooling initiatives, or public transportation options to reduce traffic congestion and emissions, these efforts may be limited in their effectiveness, particularly in remote or inaccessible locations. Furthermore, the development of infrastructure such as roads, parking lots, and access trails associated with the resort and HOA can result in habitat fragmentation, ecosystem disturbance, and loss of biodiversity.

3. **Waste Generation and Management:** Ski resorts and their associated HOAs generate significant amounts of waste, including food waste, packaging materials, and disposable products. While some resorts may implement recycling programs, composting initiatives, or waste reduction strategies, others may struggle to effectively manage their waste streams, leading to environmental contamination,

pollution, and habitat degradation. Additionally, the construction and operation of resort infrastructure may result in land disturbance, soil erosion, and deforestation, further contributing to ecosystem degradation and carbon emissions.

4. **Water Resource Management:** Snowmaking is a critical component of ski resort operations, particularly in regions with unpredictable or insufficient natural snowfall. However, the water-intensive nature of snowmaking can place significant pressure on local water resources, particularly during periods of drought or water scarcity. Ski town HOAs may be responsible for obtaining water rights, managing water usage, and ensuring compliance with environmental regulations, but these efforts may be complicated by competing interests, conflicting priorities, and limited access to alternative water sources.

5. **Climate Change Adaptation and Resilience:** As global warming continues to impact mountain ecosystems and snow-dependent economies, ski town HOAs face increasing pressure to adapt and respond to changing environmental conditions. This may include investing in renewable energy technologies, implementing carbon offset programs, promoting sustainable transportation options, and supporting ecosystem restoration and conservation initiatives. However, the effectiveness of these measures may be constrained by financial, political, and logistical challenges, as well as broader socioeconomic and cultural factors.

In conclusion, ski town HOAs can play a significant role in shaping the environmental impact of ski resorts and their associated communities. While some HOAs may prioritize sustainability, conservation, and climate resilience in their policies and practices, others may inadvertently contribute to global warming through energy-intensive operations, transportation emissions, waste generation, water resource management, and land use decisions. Moving forward, ski town HOAs must consider the long-term environmental consequences of their actions and strive to implement solutions that mitigate their impact on the planet while supporting the well-being of residents, visitors, and mountain ecosystems.

09

FARMING AGAIN ON THE HOA

In the midst of the changing landscape of HOAs, a new movement is emerging—one that challenges the traditional notions of suburban conformity and embraces the principles of self-sufficiency, sustainability, and community resilience. This chapter explores the resurgence of farming within HOA communities, where residents are reclaiming their land for small-scale agriculture, cultivating diverse crops, and fostering a deeper connection to the land and each other.

At the heart of this movement is the rebel farmer—an individual who defies the restrictive regulations of the HOA to cultivate a working farm within their property. Inspired by the ethos of homesteading and a desire for greater self-reliance, these pioneers transform their front yards into productive gardens, orchards, and micro-farms, challenging the status quo and sparking conversations about land use, food sovereignty, and community well-being. There was a man probably in they year 2018 that was breaking all the rules in the HOA in order to keep his huge yard farm in working order. He was disrupting all the so called people with power that ran the HOAs and putting in basically a glorified garden into his front yard where his grass would have been. He lived on an acre of land and he was trying to cultivate most of that land that was left after his house took up space. This was not only demising to the HOA but also to some of his neighbors that still enjoyed the cookie cutter look of every house within the neighborhood.

Since then there has been a movement for small crop yields within the HOA. In an effort to curb the displacement of water they are using that water for good and working a lot on diversification of crops to keep their soil great as well.

These small working gardens are mostly good for subsistence produce anyway. There is no way that anyone would be able to make a living on what they produce. But it is interesting that they can go back to the way of homesteading and live their life to a simple and more relaxed way of living. That is they have the leisure to pay for lower produce and have an abundance of what they already have the choices of at the grocery stores. Some front yard garden producers choosing crops that are outside of the norm giving themselves a diverse set of foods.

Anyone can put in a garden in an HOA. A lot of people are switching out their yards for gardens since their sprinklers cover most of the area anyway. This is a simple switch and one that leads to big yields.

While these small working gardens may not produce enough to sustain a livelihood, they provide a valuable source of fresh, nutritious food for residents and their families. From vegetables and herbs to fruits and flowers, these urban oases yield a bounty of flavors and aromas, enriching the culinary landscape and fostering a deeper appreciation for locally grown, seasonal produce.

By embracing drought-tolerant crops, mulching techniques, and water-efficient irrigation methods, urban farmers within HOAs prioritize water conservation and soil health. Through composting, cover cropping, and organic practices, they enrich the soil, promote biodiversity, and enhance ecosystem resilience, creating vibrant, thriving microcosms of agricultural abundance within their neighborhoods. This is not only good for the crop, but it is also good for pollinators and the flora and fauna around it. The birds and the bees love this about diverse farming and small farms. It gives them a chance at survival and revitalizes their environment and living.

Some of these farmers are looking at rain capturing systems as well as chicken coops and bee hives. As we discussed earlier in the few chapters it is a negative con on the HOAs that these people are looking at owning something that is deemed anti-aesthetic.

As the planet grapples with the escalating crisis of global warming, the role of small gardens in HOA communities takes on heightened significance. Rising temperatures, shifting weather patterns, and increasingly extreme weather events pose a direct threat to the fragile ecosystems of suburban landscapes, demanding innovative solutions and resilient practices.

In the face of rising temperatures exacerbated by the urban heat island effect, small gardens serve as vital green lungs, mitigating heat buildup, and promoting cooling through evapotranspiration. By replacing heat-absorbing surfaces with vegetation, these green spaces act as natural air conditioners, reducing energy consumption, improving air quality, and enhancing the overall livability of HOA neighborhoods. However, the rigid regulations of HOAs often impede efforts to maximize greenery, perpetuating the cycle of heat retention and exacerbating the impacts of climate change on local communities.

Beyond mere aesthetics, small gardens within HOAs play a crucial role in supporting biodiversity and ecosystem services essential for ecological balance and human well-being. By providing habitat for native plants and wildlife, these green enclaves contribute to pollinator health, pest control, and soil fertility, fostering resilient ecosystems resilient to the stresses of climate change. Yet, the narrow focus on manicured lawns and uniformity enforced by HOAs stifles biodiversity and undermines the ecological functions of green spaces, perpetuating monocultures devoid of resilience and adaptability.

In the face of mounting environmental pressures, residents within HOA communities are increasingly recognizing the need to adapt their landscapes to the realities of climate change. From xeriscaping and rainwater harvesting to permaculture and agroforestry, innovative approaches to landscaping offer sustainable solutions for mitigating the impacts of global warming while enhancing the beauty and functionality of residential environments. However, the restrictive covenants and design guidelines imposed by HOAs often hinder the adoption of these adaptive practices, impeding progress towards a more sustainable and resilient future.

Despite the challenges posed by HOA regulations, grassroots movements are emerging to empower residents and advocate for greater flexibility in landscaping policies. Through education, outreach, and collective action, residents are challenging the status quo, pushing for reforms that prioritize environmental sustainability, community resilience, and the well-being of future generations. By reclaiming their rights to cultivate green spaces that serve both ecological and social functions, residents within HOA communities are forging a path towards a greener, more sustainable future, one garden at a time.

In the midst of the changing landscape of HOAs, a new movement is emerging—one that challenges the traditional notions of suburban conformity and embraces the principles of self-sufficiency, sustainability, and community resilience. This chapter explores the resurgence of farming within HOA communities, where residents are reclaiming their land for small-scale agriculture, cultivating diverse crops, and fostering a deeper connection to the land and each other.

At the heart of this movement is the rebel farmer—an individual who defies the restrictive regulations of the HOA to cultivate a working farm within their property. Inspired by the ethos of homesteading and a desire for greater self-reliance, these pioneers transform their front yards into productive gardens, orchards, and micro-farms, challenging the status quo and sparking conversations about land use, food sovereignty, and community well-being.

Since then, there has been a movement for small crop yields within the HOA. In an effort to curb water displacement, residents are using that water for good and working on diversifying crops to maintain soil health. These small working gardens mostly produce for subsistence, but they offer residents a simpler and more relaxed way of living, with an abundance of choices at grocery stores.

While these small working gardens may not produce enough to sustain a livelihood, they provide a valuable source of fresh, nutritious food for residents and their families.

From vegetables and herbs to fruits and flowers, these urban oases yield a bounty of flavors and aromas, enriching the culinary landscape and fostering a deeper appreciation for locally grown, seasonal produce.

By embracing drought-tolerant crops, mulching techniques, and water-efficient irrigation methods, urban farmers within HOAs prioritize water conservation and soil health. Through composting, cover cropping, and organic practices, they enrich the soil, promote biodiversity, and enhance ecosystem resilience, creating vibrant, thriving microcosms of agricultural abundance within their neighborhoods.

In the face of rising temperatures exacerbated by the urban heat island effect, small gardens serve as vital green lungs, mitigating heat buildup, and promoting cooling through evapotranspiration. By replacing heat-absorbing surfaces with vegetation, these green spaces act as natural air conditioners, reducing energy consumption, improving air quality, and enhancing the overall livability of HOA neighborhoods.

Beyond mere aesthetics, small gardens within HOAs play a crucial role in supporting biodiversity and ecosystem services essential for ecological balance and human well-being. By providing habitat for native plants and wildlife, these green enclaves contribute to pollinator health, pest control, and soil fertility, fostering resilient ecosystems resilient to the stresses of climate change.

In the face of mounting environmental pressures, residents within HOA communities are increasingly recognizing the need to adapt their landscapes to the realities of climate change. From xeriscaping and rainwater harvesting to permaculture and agroforestry, innovative approaches to landscaping offer sustainable solutions for mitigating the impacts of global warming while enhancing the beauty and functionality of residential environments.

Despite the challenges posed by HOA regulations, grassroots movements are emerging to empower residents and advocate for greater flexibility in landscaping policies. Through education, outreach, and collective action, residents are challenging the status quo, pushing for reforms that prioritize environmental sustainability, community resilience, and the well-being of future generations. By reclaiming their rights to cultivate green spaces that serve both ecological and social functions, residents within HOA communities are forging a path towards a greener, more sustainable future, one garden at a time.

CHAPTER

10

LITTLE FREE LIBRARIES,
FOOD PANTRIES AND
NEIGHBORHOOD GARDENS

Homesteading seems to have made the loop after all and before we even had to make it into an effort. We seem to be sharing more than ever and in a spirit of teamwork when it comes to communities.

There are neighborhood gardens popping up all over the place for neighborhoods and churches who are an apartment complex or a bunch of condos that don't have enough space for gardens. Sometimes the HOA or regulating owner of the complex will give initiative to the people to start a free or communal neighborhood garden.

These people in charge are also giving tenants the right to own little free libraries or food pantries that sit outside of that persons house, which add to the communities life support.

Homesteading, once considered a relic of the past, has found new life in the heart of modern communities. Rather than isolationism, we're witnessing a resurgence of shared resources and collective effort. Neighborhood gardens are sprouting up in unexpected places, transforming concrete jungles into vibrant green spaces, all thanks to the collaborative spirit fostered by Homeowners Associations (HOAs) and property management companies. This may be because they are starting to get an idea of the impact of global warming and/or they are getting the idea that their rules and regulations are outdated and they need a revamping of their property licenses.

In communities where space is a premium, such as apartment complexes and condominiums, traditional gardening plots are a luxury few can afford. Recognizing this need, proactive HOAs and property managers have begun championing the establishment of free or communal neighborhood gardens. These initiatives not only beautify the surroundings but also foster a sense of belonging and community pride among residents.

Picture this: what was once a drab corner of a parking lot or unused patch of grass now bursts with life. Rows of vegetables, herbs, and flowers thrive under the care of enthusiastic residents-turned-gardeners. Neighbors come together to plant, water, and harvest, sharing in the fruits of their labor both literally and figuratively.

But it doesn't stop there. In the same spirit of generosity, HOAs and property owners are empowering residents to take ownership of other communal resources, such as little free libraries and food pantries. These small structures, strategically placed within the community, serve as hubs of connectivity and support.

Little free libraries stand as testaments to the power of literacy and community exchange. Residents donate books they've enjoyed, while others peruse the shelves for their next literary adventure. It's not uncommon to see neighbors striking up conversations over a shared favorite novel or recommending titles to one another.

Similarly, food pantries offer a lifeline to those facing food insecurity within the community. Stocked with non-perishable goods and basic necessities, these pantries provide a safety net for individuals and families in need. Whether it's a neighbor experiencing a temporary hardship or someone looking to pay it forward, the pantry ensures that no one goes hungry within the community's embrace.

Together, these initiatives weave a tapestry of interconnectedness and support, transforming neighborhoods into vibrant hubs of communal living. It's a testament to what can be achieved when individuals come together with a common purpose, supported by forward-thinking HOAs and property managers.

As the sun sets over the thriving garden beds and the pages of well-loved books, one thing becomes abundantly clear: the true wealth of a community lies not in its material possessions, but in the bonds forged between its residents. And with each seed planted and each book shared, these bonds grow stronger, enriching the lives of all who call this community home.

Church gardens have really been a home to a lot of people as well. With the community of Church for a long time being the centerpiece of the American culture, it is nice to prolong that relationship and continue forth into the world of global warming. church gardens serve as beautiful extensions of the community and provide numerous benefits beyond their aesthetic appeal. They can offer a sense of tranquility and connection to nature, creating a peaceful environment for reflection and meditation.

Moreover, in the face of climate change, these gardens can play a vital role in promoting environmental sustainability. They provide opportunities for local food production, which can help reduce carbon emissions associated with transportation and promote healthier eating habits. Additionally, they can serve as green spaces that support biodiversity, provide habitat for pollinators, and contribute to urban cooling and air quality improvement.

By nurturing these church gardens and integrating eco-friendly practices, communities can not only preserve their cultural heritage but also contribute positively to addressing the challenges of global warming. It's a beautiful way to merge tradition with contemporary environmental consciousness.

Homesteading seems to have made a comeback, not through individualism, but through a spirit of collective effort and resource sharing within modern communities. Neighborhood gardens are sprouting up in unexpected places, transforming concrete jungles into vibrant green spaces, all thanks to the collaborative spirit fostered by Homeowners Associations (HOAs) and property management companies. Perhaps this resurgence is driven by a growing awareness of the impacts of global warming or a realization that outdated rules and regulations need a revamp.

In communities where space is limited, proactive HOAs and property managers are championing the establishment of free or communal neighborhood gardens. These initiatives not only beautify the surroundings but also foster a sense of belonging and community pride among residents.

Imagine a once drab corner of a parking lot or unused patch of grass now bursting with life. Rows of vegetables, herbs, and flowers thrive under the care of enthusiastic residents-turned-gardeners. Neighbors come together to plant, water, and harvest, sharing in the fruits of their labor both literally and figuratively.

But it doesn't stop there. In the same spirit of generosity, HOAs and property owners are empowering residents to take ownership of other communal resources, such as little free libraries and food pantries. These small structures serve as hubs of connectivity and support within the community.

Little free libraries stand as testaments to the power of literacy and community exchange. Residents donate books they've enjoyed, while others peruse the shelves for their next literary adventure. It's not uncommon to see neighbors striking up conversations over a shared favorite novel or recommending titles to one another.

Similarly, food pantries offer a lifeline to those facing food insecurity within the community. Stocked with non-perishable goods and basic necessities, these pantries provide a safety net for individuals and families in need.

Together, these initiatives weave a tapestry of interconnectedness and support, transforming neighborhoods into vibrant hubs of communal living. It's a testament to what can be achieved when individuals come together with a common purpose, supported by forward-thinking HOAs and property managers.

As the sun sets over the thriving garden beds and the pages of well-loved books, one thing becomes abundantly clear: the true wealth of a community lies not in its material possessions, but in the bonds forged between its residents. And with each seed planted and each book shared, these bonds grow stronger, enriching the lives of all who call this community home.

Church gardens have also played a significant role in fostering community connections and promoting environmental sustainability. These gardens provide opportunities for local food production, support biodiversity, and contribute to urban cooling and air quality improvement. By nurturing these green spaces and integrating eco-friendly practices, communities can preserve their cultural heritage while addressing the challenges of global warming in a beautiful and meaningful way.

Chapter: Opening Up Hunting in HOA zones

Title: Opening Up Hunting in HOA Zones: Balancing Conservation, Safety, and Community Concerns

Introduction: Hunting has long been a tradition deeply rooted in American culture, serving not only as a recreational activity but also as a means of wildlife management and conservation. However, in many residential areas governed by Homeowners Associations (HOAs), hunting is prohibited due to concerns about safety, property damage, and community aesthetics. This chapter explores the contentious issue of opening up hunting in HOA zones, weighing the benefits of wildlife management and conservation against the potential risks and challenges associated with introducing firearms and hunting activities into residential communities.

The Case for Hunting in HOA Zones:

1. Wildlife Management: Hunting plays a crucial role in managing wildlife populations and promoting ecological balance. In HOA zones where deer overpopulation, nuisance wildlife, and habitat degradation are prevalent issues, controlled hunting can help mitigate these challenges and support healthier ecosystems. By reducing deer densities, hunting can alleviate crop damage, reduce vehicle collisions, and prevent the spread of diseases such as chronic wasting disease (CWD).

2. Conservation: Hunting revenue generated through license fees and excise taxes on firearms and ammunition contributes significantly to wildlife conservation efforts across the country. Opening up hunting in HOA zones could provide additional funding for habitat restoration, species conservation programs, and wildlife research initiatives. Moreover, allowing residents to participate in hunting

activities fosters a deeper connection to nature and promotes stewardship of natural resources.

3. Property Rights and Personal Freedoms: Advocates for hunting in HOA zones argue that property owners should have the right to use their land for lawful recreational activities, including hunting, as long as it is conducted safely and responsibly. Restricting hunting within HOA communities may infringe upon individual property rights and personal freedoms, particularly for residents who value hunting as a cultural or recreational tradition.

Challenges and Concerns:

1. Safety: One of the primary concerns surrounding hunting in HOA zones is the potential risk to public safety. Introducing firearms into residential areas raises concerns about accidental shootings, stray bullets, and conflicts between hunters and non-hunting residents or pets. Ensuring adequate safety measures, such as designated hunting areas, strict firearm regulations, and hunter education programs, is essential to mitigate these risks.

2. Property Damage: Hunting activities, particularly those involving firearms, may result in property damage such as stray bullets hitting homes, vehicles, or other structures. Additionally, the presence of hunters and hunting equipment (e.g., tree stands, blinds) could detract from the aesthetic appeal of the community and diminish property values. HOAs must address these concerns through effective zoning regulations, liability insurance requirements, and enforcement mechanisms.

3. Community Cohesion: The introduction of hunting in HOA zones has the potential to divide communities, with some residents supporting the initiative while others oppose it. Concerns about noise pollution, disruption of peaceful enjoyment, and conflicts between hunters and non-hunting residents may strain community relations and erode trust within the neighborhood. Building consensus through open dialogue, community engagement, and compromise is essential to maintain harmony and cohesion within HOA communities.

The debate over opening up hunting in HOA zones reflects the complex interplay between wildlife management, property rights, safety considerations, and community dynamics. While hunting can offer ecological and recreational benefits, its implementation in residential areas requires careful planning, collaboration, and risk mitigation strategies. By balancing the interests of wildlife conservation, public safety, and community well-being, HOAs can navigate this contentious issue and foster sustainable coexistence between humans and wildlife within residential neighborhoods.

You could imagine that there will be a ban on the size of the firearm, whilst the majority of the furberrers on the land will be small game, including rabbit, and squirrell, but the implimentation of bow and arrow might be appropriate for the deer.

Indeed, implementing restrictions on the size and type of firearms allowed for hunting within HOA zones could be a prudent measure to enhance safety and mitigate concerns about property damage. For small game hunting, such as rabbit and squirrel, firearms with smaller calibers and reduced muzzle velocities may be sufficient and less likely to pose significant risks to residents and property. Additionally, promoting the use of alternative hunting methods like bow and arrow for larger game such as deer can further minimize the potential for accidents and property damage.

Bow hunting offers several advantages in residential areas compared to firearms hunting. Firstly, bows have a shorter effective range than firearms, reducing the risk of stray arrows traveling beyond designated hunting areas and into residential properties. This helps mitigate concerns about safety and property damage while allowing for controlled hunting activities within HOA zones.

Moreover, bow hunting requires a higher level of skill and precision, as hunters must approach their targets quietly and accurately to ensure a humane harvest. This aspect of bow hunting promotes responsible and ethical hunting practices, fostering a greater sense of respect for wildlife and the surrounding community.

Incorporating bow hunting alongside restrictions on firearm use can provide HOAs with a balanced approach to wildlife management and conservation. By diversifying hunting methods and emphasizing safety protocols, HOAs can create opportunities for residents to engage in hunting activities while minimizing potential risks and conflicts within the community. Additionally, educating residents about the benefits of bow hunting and providing resources for hunter education and certification can further promote responsible hunting practices and enhance overall safety within HOA zones.

You could imagine that the cats and dogs sometime in the future will be a part of the wild again, and maybe this is a time to reap a piece of what we have been graced with.

Imagining a future where domestic cats and dogs revert to a wild state raises intriguing questions about the relationship between humans and animals, as well as the dynamics of wildlife management within HOA zones. While such a scenario may seem far-fetched, it prompts us to consider the potential implications and opportunities for hunting within these communities.

If domestic cats and dogs were to become feral and establish populations in the wild, it could lead to ecological imbalances and conflicts with native wildlife. In such a situation, responsible wildlife management strategies may involve implementing controlled hunting programs to manage feral animal populations and mitigate their impact on local ecosystems.

Hunting could serve as a means of population control for feral cats and dogs, helping to prevent overpopulation and reduce predation pressure on native species. By establishing hunting regulations and permitting residents to participate in targeted hunting activities, HOAs can contribute to the conservation of native wildlife while addressing the challenges posed by feral animal populations.

Moreover, hunting could provide residents with opportunities to engage in recreational activities that promote a deeper connection to the natural world. Participating in responsible hunting practices within HOA zones could foster a sense of stewardship and responsibility towards wildlife conservation, encouraging residents to play an active role in managing local ecosystems.

However, it's essential to approach the idea of hunting feral cats and dogs with caution and sensitivity. Balancing the need for population control with ethical considerations and animal welfare concerns is paramount. Implementing humane and effective hunting methods, such as trapping and euthanasia, under the guidance of trained professionals can help minimize suffering and ensure the ethical treatment of feral animals.

Furthermore, educating residents about the ecological impacts of feral animal populations and the importance of responsible wildlife management practices is essential for fostering a community-wide understanding and support for hunting initiatives within HOA zones. By promoting dialogue and collaboration among residents, HOAs can develop effective strategies for addressing emerging wildlife management challenges and safeguarding the ecological integrity of their communities.

Chapter: Setting all the animals free and on farms

Chapter: Embracing Animal Liberation on HOA Farms

In recent years, there has been a growing movement advocating for animal welfare and the ethical treatment of livestock on farms. This movement challenges conventional farming practices and calls for a paradigm shift towards more compassionate and sustainable approaches to animal husbandry. Within the context of Homeowners Associations (HOAs), which often regulate land use and agricultural activities, the concept of setting animals free on farms presents both challenges and opportunities for redefining the relationship between humans and animals within residential communities.

Animal liberation on HOA farms entails allowing animals to roam freely and express their natural behaviors, rather than confining them to restrictive enclosures or intensive production systems. This approach aligns with the principles of homesteading, where self-sufficiency and harmony with nature are central tenets. By embracing animal liberation, HOA communities can create more humane and environmentally friendly farming practices that prioritize the well-being of animals and the health of the ecosystem.

One of the key benefits of setting animals free on HOA farms is the promotion of animal welfare and psychological well-being. In traditional farming systems, animals are often subjected to cramped living conditions, confinement, and stressful management practices. By allowing animals to roam freely and interact with their environment, HOA farms can provide them with opportunities for natural behaviors such as grazing, foraging, and socializing. This not only improves the quality of life for the animals but also enhances their overall health and resilience.

Furthermore, animal liberation on HOA farms can have positive environmental impacts by promoting regenerative agriculture and biodiversity conservation. Free-roaming animals contribute to soil fertility through grazing and foraging, helping to build organic matter and improve soil structure. Additionally, they play a role in controlling weeds, pests, and invasive species, reducing the need for chemical inputs and promoting ecological balance within the farm ecosystem.

However, transitioning to animal liberation on HOA farms requires careful planning, consideration, and collaboration among residents, farmers, and HOA boards. It involves reimagining traditional farming practices and implementing alternative management strategies that prioritize animal welfare, environmental sustainability, and community engagement.

One approach to implementing animal liberation on HOA farms is through rotational grazing systems, where animals are moved regularly between paddocks to mimic natural grazing patterns and prevent overgrazing. This not only improves pasture health and productivity but also allows animals to access fresh forage and exercise greater freedom of movement.

Additionally, HOA communities can explore alternative livestock management practices such as agroforestry, silvopasture, and mixed-species grazing, which integrate trees, shrubs, and perennial crops into livestock production systems. These systems provide shade, shelter, and additional forage for animals while promoting biodiversity, soil conservation, and carbon sequestration.

Furthermore, HOAs can incentivize and support farmers who adopt animal-friendly practices through education, training, and financial assistance. By providing resources and technical support, HOAs can empower farmers to transition to more humane and sustainable farming methods while enhancing the ecological resilience and cultural richness of their communities.

In conclusion, embracing animal liberation on HOA farms represents a transformative opportunity to reimagine the future of agriculture and foster a deeper connection between humans, animals, and the land. By prioritizing animal welfare, environmental sustainability, and community collaboration, HOA communities can create thriving farm ecosystems that promote compassion, resilience, and harmony with nature.

Chapter: Shared Animal Housing in the Interstitial Spaces of HOA Communities

As the concept of animal liberation gains traction within HOA communities, residents and homeowners associations alike are exploring innovative approaches to integrate livestock into residential environments while preserving the aesthetic appeal and functionality of neighborhood spaces. One such approach involves leveraging the interstitial spaces between houses to create shared animal housing facilities, fostering a sense of community engagement and collaboration while promoting sustainable agricultural practices.

The interstitial spaces, often overlooked or underutilized areas between residential properties, present a unique opportunity to accommodate shared animal housing within HOA communities. These spaces can include alleys, backyards, green belts, and other common areas that are not typically used for housing or recreational purposes. By repurposing these spaces for communal animal shelters, HOA residents can maximize the use of available land while minimizing the impact on individual properties.

Shared animal housing facilities in the interstitial spaces of HOA communities offer several benefits, both practical and social. From a practical standpoint, these facilities can help address space constraints and zoning regulations that limit the number and type of animals residents can keep on their properties. By centralizing animal housing in designated areas, HOAs can ensure compliance with local ordinances while providing residents with access to shared resources and infrastructure.

Moreover, shared animal housing encourages collaboration and cooperation among residents, fostering a sense of community and collective responsibility for animal care and management. Instead of each homeowner maintaining separate animal shelters on their property, residents can pool their resources and expertise to create shared facilities that benefit the entire community. This collaborative approach not only promotes efficiency and cost savings but also strengthens social ties and neighborhood cohesion.

In terms of design and implementation, shared animal housing facilities can take various forms depending on the size, layout, and preferences of the HOA community. Modular structures, such as barns, coops, and shelters, can be constructed or retrofitted to accommodate different types of livestock, including chickens, rabbits, goats, and small livestock. These structures can be strategically located in central or designated areas within the community to maximize accessibility and convenience for residents.

Furthermore, shared animal housing facilities can incorporate sustainable design features and technologies to minimize environmental impact and promote resource efficiency. Solar panels, rainwater harvesting systems, and composting toilets can help reduce energy consumption, water usage, and waste generation, making the facilities more environmentally friendly and cost-effective in the long run.

However, the implementation of shared animal housing in HOA communities also presents challenges and considerations that must be addressed to ensure success and acceptance among residents. Concerns related to noise, odor, sanitation, and aesthetics may arise, requiring careful planning, communication, and consensus-building among stakeholders.

Additionally, HOAs must establish clear guidelines, rules, and protocols governing the use and management of shared animal housing facilities to prevent conflicts and ensure compliance with local regulations. This may include policies related to animal care, feeding, waste management, noise control, and community participation, as well as procedures for resolving disputes and addressing non-compliance.

Overall, the integration of shared animal housing in the interstitial spaces of HOA communities represents a promising opportunity to promote sustainable agriculture, community engagement, and social cohesion. By leveraging the collective resources and expertise of residents, HOAs can create vibrant, inclusive, and environmentally responsible communities where humans and animals coexist harmoniously for the benefit of all.

CHAPTER
11

COVID AND MY STRUGGLE WITH HOMELESSNESS

I had some trouble dealing with a bout of no work for a period of time right around Covid. I was one of the unlucky ones who were not doing well before Covid hit, and Covid just made it worse off for me just like the rest of us. That is I didn't have a job before the Covid-19 epidemic.

Also this was a time where minimalism was really changing how people were doing things with global warming taking the stage and stealing the show with buying and having very little possessions. This was an easy change for me as was with a lot of people because with Covid and not having a job, I was stressed with the fact that I couldn't buy much. But with minimalism I decided to join the ranks and be a better curb for global warming and own less. That is, own less clothes and less possessions.

So that to me was the hard part of Covid; dealing with minimalism. The easy part was making it and surviving. Whenever you are in a hard spot in life it is always key to keep your head down and make the most of that situation. So I did just that and kept my optimism for the future. I knew Covid was going to blow over and that I would soon find a job, and I did. But in the meantime I think I did well with what we had in the neighborhood. I did well with my church garden, as well as the garden at my folks house that we did some trading with, and I utilized the food pantry. All three of these things plus food stamps enabled me to get by with what I needed for food.

As with a lot of us our neighborhood and the homestead of our environment kept us alive, but it was a test on it all. It was a test to see if our community would help us out and survive and it was a test to see If our neighbor would be as open to helping us as back in the day when Ralph Waldo Emerson was alive. The most profound realization came from the collective spirit of resilience that permeated our neighborhood. Despite the challenges, we banded together, supporting one another through acts of kindness and solidarity. It was a testament to the enduring power of community in the face of adversity.

As I reflect on those tumultuous times, I am filled with gratitude for the strength and resilience of the human spirit. The trials of homelessness and unemployment may have tested our resolve, but they also brought us closer together, reminding us of the inherent goodness and compassion that resides within each of us.

In the face of uncertainty, we found hope. In the depths of despair, we found strength. And in the embrace of our community, we found a home. For it is in the darkest of times that the light of human kindness shines brightest, illuminating the path forward with hope and resilience.

It was during this time where I realized the turn around of homesteading. I read about the people growing farms on their front yard which inspired me to keep bees at one of my friends house on an HOA. It inspired me to think about the long road that HOAs have taken in order to get where they are at today. With some people hating and despising them and some people who get along great with what they do

It was during this time where I realized that even through trials and tribulations of HOAs owning the rights over us and the laws that govern our ability to survive and thrive we have persevered and made it through this. Despite the obstacles and regulations, it's inspiring to see how people continue to innovate and find ways to live sustainably and harmoniously with their communities.

During the challenging period of unemployment and navigating minimalism during the Covid-19 pandemic, I found myself faced with unexpected hurdles. Struggling to make ends meet without a job, I was thrust into a situation where owning less became a necessity rather than a choice. Despite the difficulties, embracing minimalism turned out to be a blessing in disguise. With fewer possessions, I learned to appreciate the simple joys of life and prioritize what truly mattered.

Amidst the uncertainty, my community became a lifeline. Through acts of kindness and solidarity, neighbors and friends rallied around each other, offering support and encouragement in times of need. It was in this collective spirit of resilience that I found solace and strength to persevere.

As I reflect on those challenging times, I'm filled with gratitude for the unwavering support of my community. Despite the setbacks, we came together, proving that even in the darkest of times, the light of human kindness shines through. Through shared struggles and triumphs, we forged bonds that will last a lifetime.

In the face of adversity, I discovered the power of resilience and the importance of community. Together, we weathered the storm, emerging stronger and more united than ever before. And as we move forward, I carry with me the lessons learned and the bonds formed, knowing that with the support of my community, I can overcome any obstacle that comes my way.

CHAPTER

12

GOOD AND BAD

In the end it is a challenge to see where this will end up this HOA behavior of both good and bad. On one had we have a HOA that is doing well and putting in gardens and allowing people to put in little free libraries, food pantries, bee hives, chicken coops and rain collection systems. But on the other hand there are some HOAs that don't even let a person put up solar panels let alone the rest of the items.

We have two sides of the coin. Some people who are changing with the times and some that are not wanting to budge that have control over others in a situation of ordinance and compliance. Its the Dichotomy of HOA Behaviors . But Shadows loom in the form of staunch traditionalism. In the realm of conservative HOAs, the light of progress struggles to penetrate the fortress of rigid ordinances and unyielding compliance. Here, the mere thought of solar panels evokes resistance, let alone the prospect of embracing other innovative initiatives.

This duality embodies the essence of the HOA landscape—a juxtaposition of forward-thinking pioneers and steadfast traditionalists. While some embrace change as an inevitable part of progress, others cling to familiarity, wielding control over their domain with a firm hand.

As the tapestry of HOA behavior unfolds, one cannot help but ponder the ultimate destination of this journey. Will the scales tip in favor of progress, with HOAs embracing innovation and adaptability? Or will the anchor of tradition hold fast, resisting the winds of change?

Only time will unveil the fate of HOA behavior—whether it steers towards the shores of enlightenment or remains anchored in the harbor of convention. Until then, the saga of good and bad within HOAs continues, a testament to the enduring struggle between tradition and transformation.

As urban planning and governance evolve, the role of Homeowners Associations (HOAs) may indeed undergo significant transformation. Municipal ordinances and higher levels of government regulation could increasingly shape the landscape of residential development and community standards.

HOAs have often been criticized for their sometimes arbitrary rules and enforcement, leading some to advocate for greater oversight by local governments. This shift could potentially result in more standardized regulations and a reduction in the autonomy of HOAs.

However, the future of HOAs remains uncertain. While some argue for their dissolution in favor of centralized governance, others believe in the value of community-driven decision-making and the benefits of localized management. The interplay between these perspectives, along with broader societal trends and legislative changes, will ultimately shape the fate of HOAs in the years to come.

As the dichotomy of HOA behaviors unfolds, we are faced with a profound question: where will this journey ultimately lead? On one side, we witness progressive HOAs embracing change, fostering innovation, and empowering their communities. Yet, on the other side, conservative strongholds resist the tide of transformation, clinging to tradition and control.

This juxtaposition encapsulates the essence of the HOA landscape—a tug-of-war between progress and tradition, adaptation and resistance. The path forward remains uncertain, as the scales teeter between enlightenment and convention.

As we contemplate the future of HOAs, we are reminded of the broader context of urban planning and governance. Municipal ordinances and government regulations may increasingly shape the trajectory of residential development, potentially curbing the autonomy of HOAs and standardizing community standards.

Criticism of HOAs' arbitrary rules and enforcement has fueled discussions about greater oversight by local governments. While some advocate for centralized governance, others champion the value of community-driven decision-making and localized management.

In the midst of these debates, the future of HOAs hangs in the balance. Will they evolve to meet the demands of a changing society, or will they remain anchored in tradition? The interplay of perspectives, societal trends, and legislative changes will ultimately determine the fate of HOAs in the years ahead.

As we navigate this uncertain terrain, one thing is clear: the saga of HOAs is far from over. It is a testament to the enduring struggle between tradition and transformation, a journey that continues to unfold with each passing day.

13

AI AND SINGULARITY

Singularity, where individuals have total ownership and self-sufficiency. Singularity like homesteading but only coined meaning that it will be the people who own everything individually. That is, each individual will have it all… They will have a mine in their back yards with a tool like AI to distinguish different types of minerals that they can utilize. They will have a cotton jinn in their backyards.

In the ongoing discourse surrounding global warming and its far-reaching implications, there emerges a compelling narrative of empowerment amidst crisis. The concept of Singularity, often associated with futuristic technological advancements, offers a unique perspective on how individuals can assert control and self-sufficiency in the face of environmental upheaval. As we navigate the challenges of climate change, the role of Homeowners Associations (HOAs) takes on a new dimension, serving as potential catalysts for this transformative shift.

Redefining Singularity:

Traditionally, Singularity has been portrayed as a point in the future where technological growth becomes uncontrollable and irreversible, leading to profound changes in human civilization. However, in the context of global warming and its associated challenges, Singularity takes on a nuanced meaning. It becomes a beacon of hope, signaling a time when individuals harness advanced technology to achieve unprecedented levels of self-sufficiency and resilience.

The Rise of Empowered Homeowners:

HOAs, often criticized for their stringent regulations and bureaucratic tendencies, have the potential to become agents of change in this narrative. Imagine a community where each homeowner possesses the tools and technologies to mitigate the impacts of climate change within their own property lines. From solar panels and rainwater harvesting systems to AI-powered resource management, residents are equipped to not only adapt to environmental challenges but also thrive in the face of adversity.

Decentralized Solutions for a Decentralized World:

The Singularity shift heralds a departure from centralized systems of governance and resource distribution. Instead of relying on external entities for essential services and resources, individuals take ownership of their fate. Picture a neighborhood where each backyard serves as a microcosm of sustainability, with residents cultivating their own food, generating clean energy, and recycling waste with the help of cutting-edge technologies.

Challenges and Opportunities:

Of course, the path to Singularity is not without obstacles. Issues of access, affordability, and equitable distribution of resources loom large. Moreover, the transition to a decentralized paradigm requires a fundamental shift in mindset, one that prioritizes collaboration over competition and collective well-being over individual gain.

Yet, within these challenges lie unparalleled opportunities for innovation and collaboration. HOAs, with their unique position at the intersection of community governance and individual property rights, can play a pivotal role in facilitating this transition. By fostering an environment of experimentation, education, and mutual support, HOAs can empower residents to embrace the principles of Singularity and chart a course towards a more sustainable future.

Conclusion:

In the face of global warming and its myriad impacts, the concept of Singularity offers a compelling vision of empowerment and resilience. By embracing advanced technologies and decentralized solutions, individuals within HOAs can take ownership of their destiny and forge a path towards a more sustainable and equitable future. As we confront the

challenges ahead, let us not underestimate the power of collective action and the transformative potential of empowered communities.

In the midst of the climate crisis, the notion of Singularity emerges as a beacon of
empowerment and self-sufficiency. Unlike its traditional portrayal as a futuristic technological phenomenon, Singularity in the context of global warming takes on a new meaning—a time when individuals harness advanced technology to navigate environmental
challenges and achieve unprecedented resilience.

Traditionally, Singularity has been envisioned as a point of uncontrollable technological growth. However, amidst the climate crisis, it becomes a symbol of hope—a time
when individuals use technology to achieve self-sufficiency and resilience. Imagine a future
where every homeowner has the tools and technologies to mitigate climate impacts within
their own property.

Homeowners Associations (HOAs), often criticized for their rigid regulations, have
the potential to become agents of change in this narrative. Picture a community where
residents are equipped with solar panels, rainwater harvesting systems, and AI-powered
resource management tools. HOAs can empower residents to adapt and thrive in the face
of environmental adversity.

Decentralized Solutions for a Decentralized World mean making thing work.
Singularity represents a departure from centralized systems, with individuals taking
ownership of their fate. Imagine neighborhoods where each backyard is a microcosm
of sustainability, with residents cultivating food, generating clean energy, and recycling
waste using cutting-edge technologies. This decentralized paradigm shifts power back to
the individual.

Transitioning to Singularity poses challenges of access, affordability, and equitable
distribution of resources. Yet, within these challenges lie opportunities for innovation
and collaboration. HOAs can play a vital role in facilitating this transition by fostering
experimentation, education, and mutual support among residents.

In the face of global warming, Singularity offers a vision of empowerment and resilience. By embracing advanced technologies and decentralized solutions, individuals within
HOAs can take control of their destiny and create a more sustainable future. As we confront the challenges ahead, let us harness the power of collective action and empowered
communities to pave the way towards a brighter tomorrow.

The Rise of Self-Sustainability with AI: Transforming Homesteads and HOAs

CHAPTER

14

In the face of mounting environmental challenges and shifting societal norms, the concept of self-sustainability has gained significant traction. With the aid of advanced technologies such as artificial intelligence (AI), individuals and communities are reimagining the way they interact with their environment and resources. This essay explores the rise of self-sustainability with AI, focusing on its implications for homesteads within Homeowners Associations (HOAs), the potential changes in HOA rules, and the vision of a future reminiscent of the agricultural landscape of the past.

The Evolution of Self-Sustainability:

Self-sustainability, once considered a niche pursuit, has evolved into a mainstream movement driven by concerns about climate change, resource depletion, and food security. At its core, self-sustainability entails reducing reliance on external resources and systems, and instead, cultivating a harmonious relationship with one's environment. Traditionally, achieving self-sustainability required significant manual labor, knowledge, and expertise. However, the advent of AI has revolutionized this paradigm, offering innovative solutions to enhance efficiency, productivity, and environmental stewardship.

Utilizing AI on the Homestead:

On the modern homestead, AI technologies offer a myriad of tools and applications to streamline operations, optimize resource utilization, and enhance sustainability. One such application is precision agriculture, where AI-powered drones, sensors, and satellite imagery are used to monitor crop health, detect pests and diseases, and optimize irrigation and fertilizer usage. By precisely targeting inputs based on real-time data, farmers can minimize waste, reduce environmental impact, and increase yields.

Furthermore, AI-driven predictive analytics can help homesteaders anticipate weather patterns, market trends, and crop yields, enabling them to make informed decisions and mitigate risks. Machine learning algorithms can analyze historical data to identify patterns and trends, providing valuable insights for crop planning, pest management, and resource allocation. Additionally, AI-powered robotics and automation can automate repetitive tasks such as planting, harvesting, and weed control, freeing up time for farmers to focus on higher-value activities.

In the realm of livestock management, AI-powered systems can monitor animal health, behavior, and productivity, allowing farmers to detect signs of illness or distress early and intervene proactively. For example, wearable sensors equipped with AI algorithms can track vital signs and movement patterns in livestock, alerting farmers to potential issues such as lameness or disease. Similarly, AI-driven feed management systems can optimize feed formulations based on nutritional requirements, reducing waste and improving animal performance.

Impact on HOA Rules and Regulations:

The rise of self-sustainability with AI has the potential to disrupt traditional HOA rules and regulations, particularly those related to property aesthetics, landscaping, and resource usage. Historically, many HOAs have imposed strict guidelines governing the appearance of properties, including restrictions on the installation of solar panels, rainwater harvesting systems, and vegetable gardens. However, as awareness of environmental issues grows and technology advances, there is increasing pressure on HOAs to relax these regulations and embrace sustainable practices.

In response to changing societal norms and technological advancements, some HOAs are beginning to revise their rules to accommodate self-sustainability initiatives. For example, HOAs may introduce guidelines for the installation of solar panels, allowing residents to generate clean energy and reduce their dependence on the grid. Similarly, HOAs may permit the establishment of community gardens, composting facilities, and rainwater harvesting systems, recognizing the environmental and social benefits of such initiatives.

Furthermore, HOAs may incentivize residents to adopt sustainable practices through rebates, subsidies, and educational programs. By promoting self-sustainability, HOAs can enhance community resilience, reduce environmental impact, and improve quality of life for residents. However, navigating the complexities of HOA governance and addressing concerns about property values, aesthetics, and liability remain significant challenges in implementing these changes.

Vision of a Future Agricultural Landscape:

Looking ahead, the integration of AI technology holds the promise of transforming the agricultural landscape into a diverse, resilient ecosystem reminiscent of the past. Instead of monoculture farming dominated by large-scale agribusinesses, we envision a future where small-scale, diversified farms thrive with the support of AI-driven tools and techniques.

In this future scenario, AI-powered precision agriculture enables farmers to optimize resource usage, minimize environmental impact, and enhance crop resilience. By leveraging real-time data and predictive analytics, farmers can make informed decisions about crop selection, rotation, and management, resulting in healthier soils, increased biodiversity, and higher yields. Additionally, AI-driven robotics and automation revolutionize farm labor, reducing the need for manual intervention and improving efficiency.

Furthermore, AI facilitates the transition towards regenerative agriculture practices that prioritize soil health, carbon sequestration, and ecosystem restoration. By integrating cover cropping, crop rotation, and agroforestry, farmers can enhance soil fertility, conserve water, and mitigate climate change. AI-powered soil monitoring systems provide insights into soil health and nutrient cycling, guiding farmers in implementing sustainable land management practices.

The rise of self-sustainability with AI represents a transformative shift in how we interact with our environment and resources. On the homestead, AI technologies offer innovative solutions to enhance efficiency, productivity, and environmental stewardship. However, realizing the full potential of AI in promoting self-sustainability requires addressing challenges related to HOA rules and regulations, as well as envisioning a future agricultural landscape that embraces diversity, resilience, and sustainability. By harnessing the power of AI and collective action, we can create a more sustainable and equitable future for generations to come.

CHAPTER

15

In the evolving landscape of homesteading within Homeowners Associations (HOAs), the role of artificial intelligence (AI) is increasingly central. AI technologies are not only revolutionizing the way individuals interact with their environment but also challenging existing HOA ordinances and regulations. As homesteaders embrace AI-driven solutions to enhance self-sustainability and resilience, they are confronting traditional HOA rules that may inhibit innovation and progress. This essay explores the intersection of AI, homesteading, and HOA ordinances, examining how AI-enabled initiatives are reshaping the homestead landscape and advocating for changes in HOA regulations to accommodate these advancements.

AI-Powered Solutions for Homesteaders:

AI technologies offer homesteaders a wide range of tools and applications to optimize resource management, improve productivity, and mitigate environmental impact. From precision agriculture and smart irrigation systems to predictive analytics and automated robotics, AI-driven solutions empower homesteaders to make data-driven decisions and streamline operations. For example, AI-powered drones can survey and monitor crops, identifying areas of stress or disease before they become problematic. Similarly, AI algorithms can analyze soil data to optimize nutrient application and irrigation schedules, ensuring optimal crop health and yield.

Furthermore, AI-enabled automation can enhance efficiency and reduce labor requirements on the homestead. Robotic systems equipped with AI algorithms can perform tasks such as planting, weeding, and harvesting with precision and accuracy, freeing up time for homesteaders to focus on other aspects of their operation. Additionally, AI-driven sensors and monitoring devices can track environmental conditions, animal health, and energy usage, providing valuable insights for decision-making and resource allocation.

Challenges with HOA Ordinances:

Despite the potential benefits of AI-driven solutions, homesteaders within HOAs often face challenges related to restrictive ordinances and regulations. Many HOAs have established rules governing property aesthetics, landscaping, and resource usage, which may conflict with innovative self-sustainability initiatives. For example, HOAs may prohibit the installation of solar panels, rainwater harvesting systems, or vegetable gardens due to concerns about property values, aesthetics, or perceived violations of community standards.

Additionally, HOAs may impose fines or penalties on homesteaders who violate these rules, creating a deterrent effect that discourages experimentation and innovation. As a result, homesteaders within HOAs may feel constrained in their ability to implement AI-driven solutions and pursue self-sustainability goals. Furthermore, the lack of flexibility in HOA ordinances may hinder collaboration and collective action among homesteaders who seek to share resources or implement community-wide initiatives.

Advocating for Change:

In response to these challenges, homesteaders are increasingly advocating for changes in HOA ordinances to accommodate AI-driven self-sustainability initiatives. By engaging with HOA boards, community members, and local authorities, homesteaders can raise awareness about the benefits of AI technologies and demonstrate how they can enhance community resilience and well-being. Additionally, homesteaders can work collaboratively to develop guidelines and best practices for integrating AI-driven solutions into HOA communities, addressing concerns related to aesthetics, property values, and liability.

Moreover, homesteaders can leverage data and evidence to make a compelling case for policy change, highlighting successful examples of AI-enabled self-sustainability initiatives in other communities. By demonstrating the economic, environmental, and social benefits of these initiatives, homesteaders can build support for revisions to HOA ordinances that promote innovation, sustainability, and resilience. Furthermore, homesteaders can engage with local government officials and policymakers to advocate for regulatory reforms that incentivize the adoption of AI technologies and support self-sustainability efforts within HOA communities.

Vision for the Future:

In the vision for the future, homesteaders within HOAs have overcome the challenges posed by restrictive ordinances and embraced AI-driven solutions to achieve self-sustainability and resilience. Community gardens flourish with AI-optimized crops, rainwater harvesting systems collect and store water for irrigation, and solar panels adorn rooftops, generating clean energy for homes and farms. AI-powered drones patrol the skies, monitoring crop health and detecting signs of pests or disease, while automated robots tend to fields and gardens with precision and efficiency.

Furthermore, HOAs have revised their rules and regulations to support and incentivize self-sustainability initiatives, recognizing the value of AI technologies in enhancing community well-being and environmental stewardship. Residents collaborate and share resources, forming resilient networks of support and cooperation. As a result, HOA communities become models of innovation and sustainability, inspiring others to follow suit and embrace the transformative potential of AI-driven self-sustainability.

The intersection of AI, homesteading, and HOA ordinances presents both challenges and opportunities for individuals seeking to achieve self-sustainability within HOA communities. By leveraging AI-driven solutions and advocating for changes in HOA regulations, homesteaders can overcome obstacles and realize their vision of a more sustainable and resilient future. Through collaboration, innovation, and collective action, HOA communities can harness the power of AI to enhance environmental stewardship, promote community well-being, and pave the way for a more sustainable world.

Printed in the United States
by Baker & Taylor Publisher Services

Printed in the United States
by Baker & Taylor Publisher Services